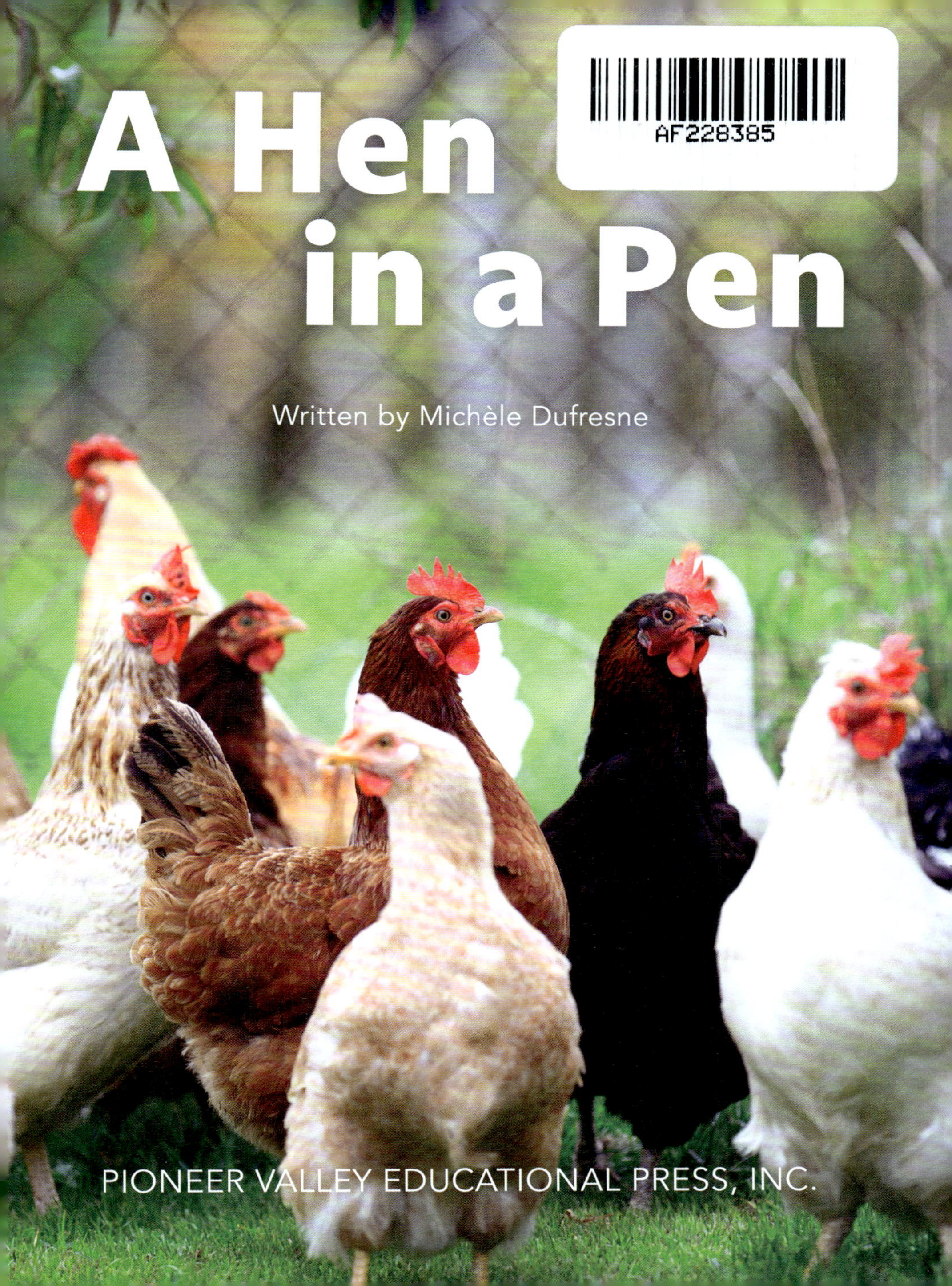

A Hen in a Pen

Written by Michèle Dufresne

PIONEER VALLEY EDUCATIONAL PRESS, INC.

AF228385

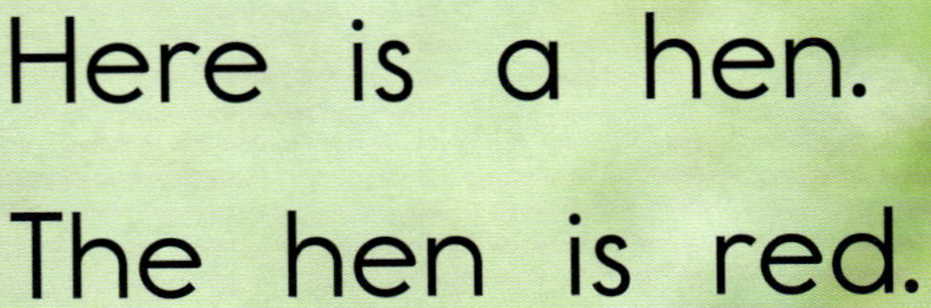

Here is a hen.
The hen is red.

Hens are female chickens.
Roosters are male chickens.

A hen can **lay** an **egg**.
Look at the eggs.

A hen can lay as many as 300 eggs a year.

Here is a hen.
The hen is in a big pen.

A big pen can keep a hen safe. The hen can get exercise and enjoy the fresh air.

I fed the hen.
Peck, peck, peck.

Hens eat anything and everything. They eat both plants and meat, so they are omnivores.

Here is a hen.
The hen is on **one** leg!

Hens often raise one foot
to rest it or keep it warm.

glossary

lay

egg

one